The Catholic Church of the Future

The
Catholic Church
of the
Future

Ernest L. Ramer

EXPOSITION PRESS   HICKSVILLE, NEW YORK

First Edition

© 1974 by Ernest L. Ramer

ISBN 0-682-48078-9

Printed in the United States of America

Contents

Introduction

In order to write any discussion of the Catholic Church of the future, it is necessary first to recognize the necessity for change and then the basic reasons for changing. Next, we must recognize the changes to be made.

The Catholic Church in the years to come will be completely changed from what it is today. The changes already made will be found to be insignificant. The leaders of the Church must realize the world cannot long continue with people believing and living as they have in the past, for the last 2000 years. Human beings themselves are already making their survival on earth much more difficult as time goes on.

Church leaders have been in disagreement over Catholic doctrine for many centuries. This proves that something is wrong either in doctrine or in belief. Errors in doctrine or belief are not the fault of God because God just does not make mistakes. So it was not God who established Catholic doctrine as it is now.

There also has been dissension among Catholic laypeople about parts of Catholic doctrine; therefore, down through the centuries many Catholics have left the Church in disagreement and confusion.

This does not mean that most Catholic leaders have not been sincere in their efforts to help Catholics in a religious way. Most Catholic leaders have tried to do their best.

Since 2000 years of effort have not produced the results that are so necessary to help the human race, something just has to be wrong. Human beings are not made wrong, because God has made every one of us just exactly as He wanted us. The only answer is that Catholic doctrine is not in complete accord with God's plan for His creatures.

The Catholic Church of the Future

CHAPTER ONE

Christ and the Catholic Church

Christ himself is the reason for the very existence of Catholic churches all over the world.

During the time Christ was preaching to the people who had gathered to listen to him, Christ told them: Unless you eat of my body and drink of my blood you shall not have eternal life.

In fulfillment of his teaching, Christ created the Holy Eucharist during the Last Supper when the twelve Apostles were with him.

The Last Supper can be considered the first Mass, because the Mass has always been the re-enactment of the changing of bread and wine into Christ's body and blood.

Therefore, the Holy Eucharist is the very heart of Catholic belief and doctrine.

During the past 2000 years members of the Catholic Church have lost the absolute faith in Christ that was shown by the twelve Apostles that Christ gathered together during His life on earth.

After Christ's death and resurrection the Apostles fully realized that Christ was truly a supernatural being sent to earth by God Himself. This faith inspired them to die rather than deny Christ. The early Christians suffered torture and death rather than give up Christ as their Master.

The process that caused the changes in belief and Catholic doctrine was gradual. The result has been that Catholic leaders have decided for themselves what Catholic doctrine should or should not be, and they have assumed the responsibility of operating the Church accordingly.

Of course, they have always had the Mass as the center of religious ceremony. This is because Christ actually established the Holy Eucharist at the Last Supper before his death. Christ instructed the apostles in unmistakable words. Taking bread, he broke it and said, "This is my Body. Do this in commemoration of Me." Then Christ took the chalice with water and wine and said, "This is my blood. Drink this in commemoration of Me. Unless you eat of my flesh and drink of my blood you shall not have eternal life."

Down through the centuries, for 2000 years, Catholic churches have celebrated the Holy Eucharist according to the command of Christ himself; they have the consecrated host of unleavened bread in the tabernacles of Catholic churches all over the world.

The reason Church leaders have had problems is that they could not agree on beliefs contained in Catholic doctrine. As a result, through the years some of the leaders broke with the Roman Catholic Church and created churches of their own, according to their ideas of belief and doctrine. So we find many Protestant churches, today, which follow Christianity as they choose.

The one way for Catholic leaders firmly to re-establish Catholic doctrine and beliefs is to go back in thought to the time of Christ and find out what Christ told the people who listened to him.

Christ was put on earth as a human being so he could tell people the truth about God.

He told his followers time and again that he was sent here to tell the people that God loved them. He told them they must believe in God in heaven. Also Christ told them they must have faith in God. They must seek the help of God rather than depend on earthly goods and pleasures.

Christ had no earthly possessions, only the robe and sandals he wore. He led a simple life and he told the people who wanted to make him king, "My kingdom is not of this earth, it is in heaven with God." Thus, Christ lived a life that was an example for human beings to follow.

Christ was crucified on the cross, not because he was a sinner, not because of the sins of people, but because he would not deny that he was the Son of God. Pilate told Christ that all he had to do was deny that he was the Son of God, and he would be released as a free man.

Christ has always been considered as the Savior of the human race. It is God who takes people into heaven. Christ can be our Savior only if we seek his help and follow him. It is up to us, not Christ.

The resurrection of Christ proved beyond any doubt that he had supernatural power and belonged with God in heaven.

The big mistake Catholic church leaders made was in their deciding what Catholics should believe, and what they should or should not do as Catholics.

Christ, by his teaching and his example, let us know what he and God in heaven expected people to do to get to heaven. Christ also said "I must do the will of My Father in heaven."

Therefore Catholic doctrine and belief must be in accordance with what Christ said and did while he was on earth.

Christ established the Blessed Eucharist at the Last Supper for just one reason: so that Christ would be present in a supernatural manner in the Catholic churches all over the world; so all could go to the Catholic church and seek the help of Christ through the Blessed Sacrament or Holy Eucharist.

It is through the Holy Eucharist that people can seek Christ's help and guidance from day to day.

Thus it is that God sent Christ to establish the Holy Eucharist in Catholic churches so that Christ would be on earth in a supernatural manner to help people.

Christ said, "Believe in God and trust him." He also said, "Follow God's will, for God's will must be done."

Therefore the most important reason for Christ's coming on earth and then creating the Holy Eucharist was to be here to help people; therefore, the Catholic Church has maintained Christ in the Holy Eucharist for nearly 2000 years.

People have kept right on living as most of them lived at the time Christ was on earth as a human being, that is, living for earthly pleasures and possessions, even though they know they must die after a limited number of years.

The reason Catholic church leaders have not influenced the lives of more people is that they, as human creatures, have declared how people should live. Man-created doctrine is subject to the errors of human beings. That is the reason for dissension among Catholic church leaders; they cannot agree on what doctrines people should believe in.

As long as human beings try to live without the help of Christ and God, world conditions will remain as they are and gradually get worse.

Human beings, because of weakness and ignorance, are created by God in such a way that they cannot earn a place in heaven with God unless they turn to God while living on earth. They must submit their wills to God's will or perish.

Thus, the basic problem of Catholic church leaders is in discovering how to make people realize that Christ and God really want to help them in their day-to-day problems of life, and then in getting these people to go to the Catholic churches to seek the help of Christ in the Blessed Sacrament of the altar.

In order to understand that God and Christ exist for the benefit of human beings, Church leaders must change the old beliefs and doctrines that are not in accordance with God and Christ.

CHAPTER TWO

God, the Master
of All His Creations

Every single star in the universe, every planet regardless of size, everything on earth has been created by God—a supernatural being, a supernatural creator.

Since the time of the first human beings, people have marveled at the wonderful creations of God. All nature conforms to God's master plan.

Awed by the wonder of nature, human beings have formulated ideas about a supernatural being: In order to prevent chaos throughout the universe, there must be a supernatural power with a master plan to maintain the orderly operation of the complete universe.

Man has found it impossible to manage the affairs of his own planet according to the way he would like. Think how much more impossible it would be for people to control the universe.

Therefore, we believe that all human beings are under the absolute control of a supernatural being, God. Scientists believe the world to be two billion years old. Throughout this time God has maintained perfect order in the operation of the earth and the rest of the universe.

Most people, if they stop and think about it, will understand the impossibility of human beings taking the place of God in the operation of the world, let alone the universe.

Just as God has an absolute plan for the operation of the

universe, so does He have a plan for people to follow during their life on earth.

The fact that people of any age do not know what life will hold for them as they go through life proves that basically people just cannot live a satisfactory life without accepting God as their master and accepting His will regardless of what happens to them.

They must accept the fact that God controls all people, and they must follow His plan for human beings.

It is only through the free will that God gave to each one of us that we can try to live our lives as we want to.

When we have a problem in life and try to solve it our way, the real opposition comes from God if our efforts are in conflict with God's plan for human beings.

Human beings are powerless to change any plan God has for the way people should live on earth.

It does not make any difference how hard or how many times man tries to do something; if it is in opposition to what God has planned for him, he cannot accomplish his goal and can only cause himself trouble, failing, finally, in his attempt to control his life on earth. God will have His way. Man has no choice but to submit to God and His supernatural power.

Because of the absolute and infallible power of God over the entire universe and all His people, the only reasonable choice any person can make is to accept God and submit his will to God's will.

CHAPTER THREE

God Created People According to His Plan

There certainly can be no question about people being created by God, a being of tremendous supernatural power. The power of God is completely beyond the greatest imagination of any human being.

No human being ever had anything to say about whether or not he should be born. He had no choice of the time or place of his birth. He had no choice of parents. He had nothing to do with whether he was to be male or female.

As a child, there was no choice of the training he would get from his parents.

These important decisions for each one of us are made through God.

It was God who created the world for all types of creatures, all types of trees, vegetables, and so on, to exist and be useful, especially for human beings.

God's plan for the creation and development of man had to be of His own making and enforcing. No one else could do it.

God created people with the kind of human nature He alone wanted.

Who made babies so weak and helpless? No one but God.

Who made children so dependent upon their parents for help in growing up? No one but God.

Who allows helpless little babies to be born to parents

who know very little about taking care of them? No one but God.

Who made people and allowed them to be so ignorant of how to live? No one but God.

Who made people so subject to sickness and disease? No one but God.

Who made people such that they could be so vicious in fighting for their own survival? No one but God.

Who made people such that they could become so discouraged and bitter about how other people treated them? No one but God.

Who made people such that they could become so deceitful and hypocritical? No one but God.

Who made people such that they would desire to seek earthly possessions above everything else? No one but God.

Who created people such that if they live long enough they become old, weak, and helpless? No one but God.

In other words God created the world with all its problems, and then created people to fight for existence the best way they could.

To look at the situation just exactly as it is, it would seem that God had put the human race in a very difficult and even impossible situation. People are born and live and finally die in the midst of problems and work and sickness, a process which usually adds up to nothing of permanent value accomplished.

The structures they build or the programs they set up are short-lived; their buildings are destroyed by man or nature and their programs are not implemented after they are dead.

It almost looks as though the lives of human beings do not have any significance. In fact, man is the most destructive force on earth. Instead of working with nature and our natural resources, too many people want to destroy what

God has put here on earth, greed being their only motive.

With conditions as we find them on earth today, with people living as they are, with people ending up in such mass confusion and lack of accomplishment, there is only one reason for God to have created the world.

The reason is that God with His supernatural power is the only being who can help and guide human beings become a contented people.

It is God alone who can and will help human beings live a wonderful life on earth, full of confidence, full of satisfaction, full of faith in Christ and God, and with complete submission of their will to God's will.

It is the lack of help from Christ and God that forces people into a miserable, hard, and meaningless life on earth.

Nothing on earth has any lasting value for human beings, even during their life.

The only real security on earth for human beings is through God and Christ.

The frightful conditions of the world are the greatest proof we can have that man needs the help and guidance of a supernatural power.

That is why Christ is present in a supernatural form in the Blessed Sacrament of the Altar in Catholic churches all over the world, just exactly as Christ wanted. The leaders of the Catholic Church must build and maintain churches for people to go to.

The presence of Christ in a supernatural form has been recognized by only a few people who have sought His help and guidance through the Blessed Sacrament. Even most Catholic leaders have failed to recognize the purpose of the presence of Christ in the Blessed Sacrament. The purpose of the presence of Christ is to help and guide any person who asks for help and then submits his will to the will of Christ and God.

CHAPTER FOUR

God and Human Nature

God is the creator of not millions, but billions of people on just the earth, alone, that we all live on.

In order to understand what human nature is truly like, we must take a good look at the great majority of God's people, as we can find them today in the world around us.

What are some of the most important characteristics of human beings? Which characteristics will be found in people regardless of the place in the world where they are living?

Babies are created as God wanted them; weak, ignorant, and much more helpless than other animals in babyhood.

They depend absolutely on their mother for care as they gradually grow stronger and develop as human beings are supposed to according to nature and God's plan.

Babies show a characteristic of fear of the unknown. Also, they display the effects of fear when they have had a bad experience with another person, or after something has scared or hurt them.

Through instinct, as provided by God in His creation of human beings, a baby feels secure and is not afraid when cuddled in his mother's arms. As the child grows and learns to walk, he still feels safe and secure as long as he can run to his mother and get her to hold him, when anything scares him. Satisfied, in the arms of his mother, the baby reveals the extreme difference between fear and confidence. The same effects are seen in children as they grow up.

As they grow older they learn to do more things for themselves, but the basic characteristics of fear and confidence remain in their minds. Even as adults and through their entire lives, people are controlled to a very great degree by their fears and by the confidence they can establish in themselves and other people who are able to help them when they are in trouble and need encouragement and consolation.

We can see how fear and trust and confidence can dominate human beings and control their actions. If we are afraid we cannot act, we automatically send the message to our subconscious mind. Our body gets the message and we cannot do it, whatever it may be. Now if we believe we can do something, the message is sent to do the thing we want to do. Thereby our subconscious mind automatically seeks a way of performing the act.

Even if we fail to accomplish what we tried to do, the mind is ready to try again what it could not do the first time. If we receive encouragement from other people who are trying to help us, we usually can learn to do what we want to do. This is the way faith or confidence works on the mind and body.

God created His creatures so that faith and confidence would be of tremendous help in their learning to do many things.

One step further and we will begin to understand that faith in God is of the greatest importance to human beings. As people learn to think for themselves they begin to understand the difference in power and knowledge between people and God.

There is no doubt that the accomplishments of people to do those things within the realm of possibility of human achievement have come about through the faith and confidence they have developed in themselves.

Great achievements in worldly goals usually come only after many years of hard work, many failures, many disappointments, and much sacrifice. Faith and confidence are absolutely necessary and must always be present in the minds of people who finally achieve their earthly goals.

We have only to look around us to see many examples of successful people in earthly things. Also, we can look around and find a much larger number of people who just cannot seem to be successful in their earthly endeavors. I wonder just how much faith and confidence they have in what they are trying to accomplish?

Since God is the creator of all human beings, He alone is responsible for the basic human behavior that is found in all God's creatures.

Through God, every person starts his life on earth as a very weak and ignorant human being. Every baby, even before birth, is almost completely dependent on its mother for help in getting everything it needs to keep alive and to grow as it should.

From his mother's teaching the baby learns to help himself in eating, walking, talking, etc. Usually the mother teaches the baby love and understanding and gives him the feeling of being wanted.

If human beings are responsible for every act of their lives to God Himself, why is it that God puts tiny babies under the control of weak and ignorant parents?

The only answer is that God does not allow babies to be born until the parents are old enough to know that God is their creator and master, who has complete control over all He has created.

God has given parents and adults the intelligence that is necessary for them to seek the help of Christ and God. It is not hard for adults to understand the tremendous and absolute power of the unknown, unseen supernatural power that rules the universe.

When a mother seeks the help and guidance of Christ

and God, instead of other people, she has faith and confidence that she will receive help in caring for her infant baby. With faith in God, a mother is able to raise her child in complete confidence that Christ and God will allow whatever is best to happen to her baby. Therefore, she can go ahead and raise her child with complete faith and confidence. The mother's faith and confidence is automatically passed on to her tiny baby.

This faith and confidence of human beings is utilized by people to the highest and most perfect degree only when they learn to depend on the help and guidance of the supernatural power of Christ and God to help them through life.

CHAPTER FIVE

God's Reason
for Sending Christ on Earth

Why would God send Christ on earth when He knew what ignorant and worldly people would do to Christ while he was on earth? It certainly was not to punish people because they were worshipping false gods and living a life of earthly luxury. It was not to free the people who were forced to serve the Romans as slaves and being treated like animals.

Was God punishing Christ by allowing him to be humiliated, scourged, tortured, and finally murdered on the cross? Certainly this was not the way God treats any of His creatures.

The birth of Christ as a human was according to God's plan for the human race. Christ was born at a time when people were confused about who created people and the world. As a result they believed in many gods and also worshipped idols of their own making. Their beliefs about these gods were that when anything happened that was harmful, the gods demanded appeasement because they were angry at the people about something.

The Jews believed in God as told of in the Old Testament. They believed that God had condemned the whole human race, from Adam and Eve on down through the ages, to a life of hardship and death because of the original sin of Adam and Eve.

If God loved His son, Christ, how could He blame Christ

for all the so-called sins of the human race from Adam and Eve on down to the coming of Christ on earth?

How could God have sent Christ to earth so a few people could hate him so much that they would murder Him to avenge the sins of Adam and Eve.

How could God in His love for His creatures, send Christ to earth to be murdered so that God would open Heaven to all people?

If God in his anger at Adam and Eve for eating forbidden fruit closed heaven to all people, why should He send Christ to earth so that a few jealous and vicious people could torture and murder him. Would God be appeased for the disobedience of Adam and Eve in eating the apples, and reopen heaven to people? What had Christ done in heaven to deserve such treatment? How could God open heaven to people who murdered Christ, when He had closed heaven to people because Adam and Eve had eaten the apples?

Prophets from time to time had predicted that a redeemer would be sent by God to redeem the human race.

St. John the Baptist had foretold that Christ would be the redeemer. So he helped prepare the people to believe Christ had come to redeem them.

God certainly had a mission for Christ on earth. Our reasoning power tells us the most important purpose God could have had was for Christ to tell people the truth about God in heaven.

Christ had to be a human being in order to talk to people and show them by his example how people should believe in God and trust in Him.

Christ told people he was the Son of God, sent by God to teach people to believe in God as the supernatural Creator of everything.

Then Christ told his listeners: love your neighbor. Forgive your enemies, seven times seventy and even seventy times seventy.

Just think of these words of Christ as compared to those of the God of the Old Testament who gave Adam and Eve only one chance *not* to eat the apples from the forbidden tree. Consider the terrible punishment wrought by God on the whole human race beginning with Adam and Eve. God was supposed to condemn Adam and Eve to suffer and die on earth instead of living in Paradise forever in ease and comfort and pleasure.

God certainly wanted to have Christ tell people the truth that He did not condemn Adam and Eve to death because they disobeyed Him. People must live and die on earth just exactly as they do because God planned it that way to begin with.

Instead of revenge and punishment and suffering, God wants to give His supernatural help to His creatures. If God treated Adam and Eve as the Bible states, how could Christ or anyone expect people to have faith in God and trust Him. They would run away from God in fear instead of seeking God's help.

So Christ preached to the people: have no fear of God. Have faith in God and when you die you will enter heaven with Him.

As Christ told people, "I must do the will of My Father in Heaven," so must people on earth submit to the will of God in heaven.

Instead of Christ dying on the cross for the sins of all people, Christ was crucified and died on the cross because he would not deny he was the Son of God.

He had preached that he was sent by his Father in heaven. The courage and strength it took Christ to suffer the crucifixion on the cross came from his faith in God. His resurrection after three days in the tomb, proved to his

Apostles beyond any doubt that Christ was actually the Son of God.

Before his death Christ called together his disciples for the Last Supper. At this time he instituted the Blessed Sacrament. He broke bread and had wine in the chalice. He told the apostles, "This is my Body and my Blood. Do this in commemoration of Me."

The Mass in the Catholic Church is based on the Last Supper by Christ and the establishment of the Blessed Sacrament. It is the changing of the bread and wine into Christ's body and blood.

The founding of the Catholic Church was an important part of Christ's mission on earth. He told his Apostles to go forth and teach all nations. At this time Peter was named head of the Church and was made the first pope of the Church.

This is the way God sent Christ to earth to establish the Catholic Church with Christ present in a supernatural way in the Blessed Sacrament.

It cannot be proved in an earthly way that the priest actually changes the bread into Christ's body and the wine into his blood. Also it cannot be proved that Christ is *not* present in a supernatural form in the Blessed Sacrament.

There is no other place in the world except in Catholic churches where the Blessed Sacrament is kept on the altars day and night, at all times. Christ did not tell people he would come to them. People must go to Christ for help. There must be some place for them to find Christ. That is why Christ is present in a supernatural manner in the Blessed Sacrament of the Altar in Catholic churches.

So we certainly can believe Christ could be present in a supernatural way in the Blessed Sacrament of the Altar. The only way people can be absolutely sure that Christ is present, some way unknown to human beings, is to go to the Catholic

church where the Blessed Sacrament is kept. If you are look-
ing for Christ in an earthly way he won't seem to be there.
But if you seek his help and sincerely believe in him you
cannot but receive his supernatural aid in some way.

Those people who doubt Christ is present certainly won't
get help from Christ.

The most important reasons for Christ's being on earth
are, first, to tell people to have faith in God and then to seek
His help; next to establish the Catholic Church; and, last, to
be present in the Catholic church in a supernatural form, unseen by human eyes, but still there to help anyone who seeks
his help.

These are the basic reasons why God sent Christ to earth
as a human being.

The crucifixion of Christ, followed by his resurrection
after three days proved he was a supernatural being.

The miracles performed by Christ proved that those people who believed sincerely and with great faith were the
people for whom Christ did so much.

Today through the Blessed Sacrament, Christ is waiting
to give those who have faith in him and God all the help they
need to enjoy a wonderful life on earth plus a reward after
death.

CHAPTER SIX

Doctrines That Will Be Changed

1. *Infallibility of the Pope*

This is a doctrine or belief that has caused trouble in the Church for many centuries. There is no question or doubt that Christ named Peter the head of the Catholic Church while Christ was on earth as a human being.

Jesus said to Peter ". . . And I say to thee, thou art Peter and upon this rock I will build my Church and the gates of hell shall not prevail against it. And I will give thee the keys of the kingdom of heaven; and whatever thou shalt bind on earth shall be bound in heaven, and whatever thou shalt loose on earth shall be loosed in heaven." Through these words Christ expressed his faith in Peter, knowing Peter would make a good leader of the Catholic Church.

Without a leader of the Church there would be no development. Someone had to do the work necessary for churches or places of worship to be built, where Mass could be performed, and where people could receive the Blessed Sacrament in Holy Communion. Christ commanded the Apostles to do as he had done at the Last Supper, just before his crucifixion.

In Rome the Christians or followers of Christ were forced to go under ground in the catacombs under the city. There the Mass was celebrated and people received Holy Communion where the Romans could not find them. Christians were killed by the Romans when they were captured, so they had to gather in secret.

So the Apostles, with Peter as their leader, did go out and establish churches in many different parts of the world. If God would have sent Christ to earth to turn over his power and God's power to Peter and all the future popes of the Church, Christ would have had a short mission on earth.

There would not have been the Last Supper with the establishment of the Holy Eucharist. There would have been no crucifixion of Christ. There would have been no death nor resurrection of Christ. Nor would there have been any appearances of Christ as a supernatural being after his resurrection.

None of these important events would have been necessary if the popes of the Church were to take the place of Christ and God on earth in helping Catholics get to heaven and be with God.

There would have been no errors in doctrine and belief or errors in helping people find Christ and God, if the popes were given the power of infallibility. Peter, as an infallible pope, would have taken care of establishing and building the churches and gathering church members into congregations. Also Peter would have determined Catholic doctrine and beliefs.

Christ would just have been a messenger sent by God to give God's power to Peter. If this was the way God wanted it, Christ's life would have been entirely different. Christ, in fairness to his followers, would have stressed time and again in his sermons that God would turn over His supernatural powers to Peter, as first pope of the Catholic Church yet to be established. Then Christ would have told his followers that all future popes of the Catholic Church would have the same powers as Peter, the first pope.

If Christ had declared infallibility for Peter and all future popes, certainly Christ would have made this known to all his followers, without any question or doubt. But Christ did not tell his followers in his sermons that popes would be infallible as leaders of the Catholic Church. That was not the purpose of Christ's coming to earth.

Peter did as Christ told him and did help to build Catholic churches. Peter and the rest of the Apostles adhered to what Christ had told them at the Last Supper and used the Mass in changing bread and wine into Christ's body and blood.

Herein lies the basis for Catholic belief and doctrine according to Christ himself.

The absolute power of the popes to rule the Church and its leaders is not to be questioned. The error would come in believing that a pope *takes the place of Christ or God* in determining how people should live on earth to satisfy God and Christ.

When Christ established the Holy Eucharist he said, "Unless you eat of my flesh and drink of my blood in the Holy Eucharist, you shall not have eternal life." This statement should prove that weak and ignorant human beings cannot get to heaven without the help of Christ and God.

This certainly does not mean that Christ turned over his supernatural power to Peter to help people get to heaven.

The power and duties of the pope lie in maintaining and operating Catholic churches all over the world. Any organization must have a leader with the proper authority to see that the organization works properly to get the job done.

In the past 2000 years since Christ, reason and history tell us that all popes were not perfect and did not act in accordance with the teachings of Christ himself.

Human beings are born and live in such ignorance and weakness that God could not turn over His responsibility and power to a mere human being, under any condition, at any time.

What did Christ tell his Apostles and other listeners?

Christ said, "I am sent by My Father in heaven to tell you to believe in Him and have faith in Him. Put away your earthly treasures and pleasures and follow God in heaven. I am here to do the will of God in heaven."

Therefore, our own reasoning power, as well as history recorded in the writings of the Apostles of Christ, lets us understand that Christ and God are the absolute and infallible powers to give supernatural help to all of God's people on earth.

2. *The Bible*

The Bible, even though it is used in many parts of the world today, does not contain the answer to the problems of people who wish to live according to God's plan for His creatures.

Many people believe the Bible is the word of God. Yet, would God direct the writing of a book that is so confusing and hard to read as the Bible? God creates people weak and ignorant; one needs only to look around to understand these important characteristics of all human beings. It would be a great injustice on the part of God to direct the writing of a book that is so confusing and hard to understand.

The Old Testament was written or passed on some way by people who lived at that time. The New Testament was written by some of the Apostles of Christ.

Many times since the first Bible was put together in book form, people have rewritten it to better explain it or to change it or to improve it. So even if God did reveal how to write the Bible, who knows how many changes have been made by now, after many centuries.

Supposing God demanded people to read the Bible and to follow it in order to get to heaven. What would God do to people who don't have a Bible, or can't read or who are blind? How would He punish them?

What if people who rewrite the Bible change it and make it different. How will God punish those who don't understand what God might have wanted in the beginning?

The Bible is more of a history of the human race since Adam and Eve than a history of God or a code of living set forth by God.

Just as no human being can take the place of God in helping other people, neither can any book take the place of God or Christ in helping people.

The Bible is probably used by so many people because it is the only means they can find to try to get some understanding of God and Christ. It is the only tool they have to use in religion. At least that is the way they feel about it. The fact remains these people have not learned how to seek the help and consolation of Christ and God.

People must seek supernatural help by asking Christ and God for guidance, help, and consolation directly, not by reading the Bible or by any other method.

3. *Church Doctrine on Sin*

The doctrine or teaching of mortal and venial sins is in error according to the teaching of Christ himself. Christ said, "Love your neighbor, do not harm him. Forgive your enemy seven times seven yes and seventy times seven."

With these statements Christ does not portray God as being the way God is supposed to be in the Old Testament. Christ certainly did not say "an eye for an eye and a tooth for a tooth."

Something is wrong when it is written in the Bible God condemned Adam and Eve to a life of suffering and, finally, death because they ate apples from a tree God had told them not to eat from. They were to have lived in Paradise in comfort and ease forever. But they were punished. And worse yet, God was supposed to have punished all the rest of the human race from then on because Adam and Eve disobeyed Him by eating the forbidden fruit.

Either Christ is wrong about God or else the Bible misrepresents God in the Old Testament.

History, recent enough to be reliable, tells a good enough story about Christ to prove to us that what Christ said about God is the truth. Christ said, "God loves you and wants you to live in Heaven with Him. But you must have faith in God and trust Him. You must submit your will to God's will. You must seek God's help."

So the leaders of the Catholic Church must follow Christ's words about God and ignore the story about Adam and Eve and their original sin.

Christ did not say it was a mortal sin to miss Mass on Sunday without a good reason. He did not say we would go to hell for missing Sunday Mass deliberately, unless we went to confession and repented, and the priest forgave our sins.

When human beings commit a serious wrong, the problem is not that we offend God. The tragedy falls on us not God. We suffer because we have not followed God's will, and because other people make us suffer. We suffer from mistakes we make because we are weak and ignorant human beings. God knows we are weak and ignorant because He created us just exactly that way. So God knows how we will make these mistakes and has no reason to get angry at us.

God gave us a conscience to guide us in choosing right from wrong, but still we are weak and ignorant.

That is the reason Christ came on earth: to tell us to seek the help of God when we are in trouble.

The meaning of the words "good and evil" will be changed. The truth is that God, in all of His creations, has provided a purpose for everything He creates. God has not given the human race the reason why He created everything in the universe just exactly as it is. Since God is master of the universe and every thing in the universe, He is the director and guiding force of everything. Therefore, everything that God does or permits to occur is positive action for good.

Evil is a misunderstood word, for God is not in heaven waiting to punish people who do not obey Him.

In the Church of the future, the word "evil" will be changed to mean the actions of people who have not followed God's plan for the human race.

People get into trouble, not because they have offended God, but because they have not accepted God as their supreme master and creator. Therefore people go about blindly seeking to do things their way instead of seeking the help of God.

The expression "good and bad people" will be discontinued. People will be divided into two groups. One group will live as weak and ignorant people who are trying to grab everything they can of earthly pleasures and material things.

The other group will be those who recognize God as their creator and absolute master on this earth and for the future after death. They will accept the events of their life as being under the control of God. By submitting their will to God's plan for them, they will receive the supernatural help of God and Christ.

The lifetime goal of these people will be to place Christ and God in the center of their life, with all things considered as the will of God and each day bringing them one day closer to their union with God in heaven. Their purpose in life will be to serve God completely and seek His help in day-to-day living on earth.

4. *The Marriage Doctrine*
As a result of very strict doctrine on marriage many Catholics have left the Church. We still are dealing with weak and ignorant people.

In the Church of the future, a study of the whole situation concerning marriage will be made. Marriage is a lifetime job for a man and his wife, involving bringing other human beings into this world. To raise these children according to God's plan is a most important obligation of parents.

Marriage will not be entered into without first a thorough study of marriage by the man and woman. This course will be given by well-qualified priests and a definite syllabus will be followed.

A six-months' training course will be provided by the Church, helping to prevent hasty marriages that will not last because people are not suited for each other. After six months of learning about married life, and at the same time six months of courtship, the man and woman will be much better able to decide about marriage and family life.

5. *The Problem of Divorce*

This is a serious problem that must be faced by many married couples.

It seems reasonable to assume the six-months study period and courtship will make for better marriages and very few divorces. Also, because of the relationship established through giving the course, priests will be better prepared to counsel people who are having trouble with their marriages.

A six-month period of counseling by the priest and attempts to improve the marriage would seem to be necessary before any steps could be taken to consider a divorce. Maybe another six-months' trial separation could help decide if the marriage could be saved. Counseling by the priest could be carried on during this next six-month period.

6. *Confession*

It is not up to the priest to forgive our wrong doings. That is something for God to decide. Christ told us to forgive our neighbor seventy times seven times. So I am sure God will forgive us.

Confession provides a wonderful opportunity for the priest to counsel and maybe advise people who need help with their problems. Of course the individual must go to Christ in the Blessed Sacrament to seek the supernatural help of Christ and God. But the priest would have a good opportunity to lead to Christ through confession. It should be a voluntary act by the individual to tell the priest in confession what his problems are. Telling problems to someone they can trust seems to be helpful to human beings.

7. *Good and Evil People*

The teaching that good people go to heaven and bad people go to hell will be stopped.

It will be replaced by church leaders teaching people that every human being must seek the help of Christ in the Blessed Sacrament of the altar. It is only through supernatural help that people can live a satisfactory life on earth. It is only our faith in Christ and a God with supernatural power that can carry us through life His way.

So only good comes from God. When we seek the help of Christ and God we are dealing only in good results. Again, only good comes from God. There is no evil connected with Christ or God.

So instead of good and bad people we have on one hand people who turn to Christ and God and submit their wills to God.

The others are not bad people. They are simply people who don't seek Christ or God. They seek the help of other people or try to do things for themselves. They are the disappointed and the discouraged.

8. *Problems with Sex Attitudes*

The old idea that we are born in sin will be discarded. Nothing that God creates is sinful in itself and no one else but God created sex in people.

Sex problems will be discussed and solved according to truth and reality, and according to God's plan for sexual activity among human beings.

9. *The Situation Concerning the Blessed Mother of Christ*

The virginity of the mother of Christ is something that can't be proved one way or another. Because Christ was born through Mary, his earthly mother, does not mean the rest of the human race is born in sin. We are all born just exactly as God wants us to be born.

The true importance of Mary is that God chose her to be the earthly mother of Christ. Mary in heaven is now a supernatural being with God.

There is no question about the value of Mary in helping human beings on earth. Many people have prayed to her for help and received supernatural help from Mary, the Mother of Christ.

At this time the Lourdes, France, shrine, Our Lady of Lourdes, is a most astounding example of supernatural help through Mary. The miracles cannot be denied because there is so much physical proof of people who have been cured by bathing in the water.

The Church should stress the real value of Christ's Mother in helping people on earth. That is most important, and people with faith will receive Mary's help.

10. *Baptism*

Baptism will take on a new meaning rather than that of the remission of original sin from Adam and Eve. The idea that only a person (even babies) who is baptized in the

Catholic Church can enter heaven with God will be eliminated.

Baptism is useful as a means of bringing babies and others into the Catholic Church. It could be used because Christ was baptized by John the Baptist as a matter of ceremony, not as a vital doctrine of the Church.

11. *Redemption*

The doctrine concerning our redemption from the sin of Adam and Eve through Christ is in error.

Christ did not die on the cross because of the effects of Adam and Eve's sin of eating the apple. Christ did not open heaven to human beings by appeasing God for the original sin of Adam and Eve.

God has never been angered by the human race. He did not send Christ on earth because He was angry with people. God sent Christ on earth to tell people that God loved them and wanted to help them. God's commandment to people is to put their faith in Him and to submit their will to His will.

Christ is God's representative on earth in a supernatural manner in the Blessed Sacrament of the Altar.

The only redemption of human beings through Christ's crucifixion could be that of the redemption of fear about God and heaven. Through Christ's crucifixion and resurrection, he proved to human beings that he was the Son of God and that life after death is possible for people.

Also Christ proved his supernatural power beyond any doubt to any person who wanted to believe in Christ.

The Apostles demonstrated this redemption from human fear after the resurrection of Christ from the dead. They went out and preached about Christ without fear of any kind, not even death itself. Christ meant so much to them, they would die rather than deny Christ or give up their faith in Christ.

The Apostles were redeemed from the bonds of human nature only after they witnessed the crucifixion of Christ and then his resurrection from the dead. It was only a supernatural being who could perform in such a manner. Since they had to believe Christ had risen from the dead, they had to follow his teachings and believe in him.

We can consider Christ as our Redeemer because he gave us the knowledge that God in heaven wants us to enter heaven with Him. But our only way is for us to believe in God and submit our will to God's will. Also, Christ will help us get to heaven through his help in the Blessed Sacrament of the Altar.

The Church would benefit very much by either eliminating the foregoing doctrines or changing them to agree with the teachings of Christ while he was on earth.

Lay members of the Church should study the life of Christ; then they would understand the mystery of the Blessed Sacrament much easier.

CHAPTER SEVEN

The Basic Future Belief of the Catholic Church

The Church of the future will center around one basic belief—the belief that Christ is present in a supernatural manner in the Blessed Sacrament of the Altar.

Christ himself created the Blessed Sacrament the night of the Last Supper before he was taken captive by the Roman soldiers. This is the first proof we can find that connects Christ to the Blessed Sacrament.

Why would God want Christ to be on earth in a supernatural manner in the Blessed Sacrament of the Altar in all Catholic churches? God wants Christ in the Blessed Sacrament on earth in Catholic churches for just one reason. The reason is that people who want the help of Christ can go to Catholic churches anywhere in the world and receive the supernatural help of Christ himself.

Every person on earth could live a more satisfactory life if he could go where Christ is present in a supernatural way. This was one thing Christ emphasized so many times. He told his followers they must have faith in him and trust him. If a person does not have true faith in Christ, he will not get much help.

Most people just cannot believe that in some way, unseen and unknown, Christ is actually present in the Catholic Church in the Holy Eucharist. So they don't visit the church when they need help.

So it was, too, when Christ was on earth as a human being. People just could not believe he was the Son of God in heaven.

They could not understand the miracles Christ performed for people who had true faith in him. How could there be greater proof of how Christ will help those who put their faith and trust in him?

A very important reason why people don't understand about the help Christ will give them is that they can only judge whether their prayer for help is *apparently* answered or not.

Almost always they will ask for something they want to get or to accomplish. They have only earthly eyes and desires. People do not know for sure if the thing they are asking for is good for them in the end, or after they get it.

If Christ is to truly help supplicants, then he can't in justice, help them obtain what is not good for them. So the result is, people pray and pray to get something they want, and then they do not get it.

If you understand Christ and God you will realize that Christ and God are certainly more intelligent than people and that Christ will know what is best. If people pray sincerely for something and do not get it, they must realize that Christ has something much better in store for them. Christ will never fail to do the best for people. Your faith is truly strengthened when you don't receive what you have prayed for; you tell yourself everything is all right; you will get something else, better yet, but you must trust Christ in spite of the fact that you did not get what you asked for.

After nearly 2000 years of trying to convert the world to follow Christ and God, the Catholic Church should finally recognize the truth: that human beings just cannot convert the world to God and Christ. No person or persons can take the place of Christ in the Blessed Sacrament of the Altar in helping people during their life on earth.

Christ himself is the only one who created the Holy Eucharist or Blessed Sacrament, so there is no better proof of Christ's wanting to help people.

How much value can the Catholic Church have for people if it cannot help people when they are in serious troubles? It is when a person needs help badly that Christ becomes all important to him in the Blessed Sacrament.

When Christ told the Apostles he would be with people until the end of time, that is just exactly what he meant.

The only difference between the time Christ was on earth and today is that today Christ is present in all Catholic churches all over the world in the supernatural manner of the Blessed Sacrament.

Leaders of the Catholic Church have no choice but to build Catholic doctrine around the supernatural presence of Christ in the Blessed Sacrament.

This means they must teach Catholics to come to church and visit Christ in the Blessed Sacrament when they are in need of help.

The exposition of the Blessed Sacrament will become a daily service for Catholics as well as non-Catholics. Any person with sincere intentions may come and visit him for help and consolation. Every person who is sincere in asking Christ for help will leave the Church feeling better than when he came. Every sincere person will receive supernatural help from Christ himself.

It does not make any difference what the problems of human beings may be, Christ is there to give the help necessary to bear the burden or to dispose of the problem.

Just think how important this is to priests who are sincerely interested in helping those people who need the help of Christ so badly.

When a person comes to them, needing help, they can go with that person into the church where the Blessed Sacrament is and pray with the person needing help. The priests can be assured Christ will help this person in need.

In the Church of the future, priests in their Sunday sermons will explain to their parishioners how people should seek the help of Christ. They will explain how necessary it is for people to have faith in Christ and to accept whatever comes from their visit to Christ in the Blessed Sacrament. The greater their faith in Christ, the easier it is to accept his will and God's will. When a person trusts Christ to help him he must take what comes.

If a person is asking for help in sickness, he must remember that the sickness may not be cured, so he asks Christ for whatever is best. It is this trust and faith in Christ that enables a person to leave the Church with a wonderful feeling of relief. This person knows that Christ will do whatever is best for him. This person also knows no person on earth could do for him what Christ can and will do.

The assurance that what is best for him will happen is a tremendous mental uplift for a human being.

This help of Christ is vital in helping people solve any important problem. Such a problem may involve a person who is planning to be married. Should he get married or not. This is a problem of tremendous importance. Again, any person can go to Christ in faith and sincerity and he will get the supernatural help of Christ in solving his problem. He can realize with absolute assurance that if he gets married it will be according to the will of Christ and God. Or if he doesn't get married, it, too, is for the best and is according to the will of Christ and God.

Either way it happens there will be no disappointment later on. Christ and God never make any mistakes. It is weak and ignorant people who make all the mistakes.

It is impossible to realize how much satisfaction priests will enjoy by teaching people to seek the supernatural help of Christ himself.

Christ and God will be put in their proper relationship with human beings. When people trust Christ and God, they place the responsibility of their well-being right in the hands of the supernatural power of both Christ and God. So it is impossible for people not to get along all right with supernatural help.

Instead of becoming discouraged and finally abandoning the mistaken doctrines established by human beings, people who seek the help of Christ in the Blessed Sacrament will find their faith becoming stronger and stronger. The more help Christ gives them, the more they will depend on him for everything they need.

Every person must learn for himself how wondeful Christ will be for those who believe in him and trust him to help them. No human being can explain this to them.

God will allow people to try to help themselves as long as they want to, but they must suffer the consequences of their ignorance and helplessness due to human nature. Remember God created people weak and ignorant because He wanted them that way. The power and strength necessary for them to enjoy a wonderful life on earth can come only from Christ and God.

Because God made man so he could choose for himself, man must seek the help of Christ in the Blessed Sacrament in Catholic churches. Neither Christ nor God are going to seek out people in order to help them. Our intelligence tells us we are created by the supernatural power of God. That is why we can understand that Christ or God, alone, can truly help us.

Therefore, Christ in the Blessed Sacrament of the Altar in Catholic churches is ready and willing to give any help needed to those people who sincerely seek his help and will submit their will to his and God's will instead of that of human beings.

CHAPTER EIGHT

The Mass of the Future

The future will bring changes in the Mass. The theme of the Mass will not be one of offering Christ's body and blood to God in atonement for the sins of Adam and Eve and the whole human race. Christ did not die on the cross to satisfy the anger of God in heaven against all of His people on earth, so that God would open heaven for His people.

During his sermons Christ told his listeners, "I am the bread of life. He who comes to Me shall not hunger, and he who believes in Me shall never thirst. But I have told you that you have seen Me and you do not believe." Another time Christ said, "I am the living bread that has come down from heaven so that if anyone eat of it he shall not die. If anyone eat of this bread, he shall live forever; and the bread that I will give is my flesh for the life of the world."

Again Christ told his followers in words that were very clear: "Amen, Amen I say to you unless you eat the flesh of the Son of Man, and drink his blood, you shall not have life in you. He who eats my flesh and drinks my blood, abides in me and I in him. As the living Father has sent me, and as I live because of the Father, so he who eats me, he shall also live because of me. This is the bread that has come down from heaven."*

After this many of Christ's followers left him. Then Christ

---

*Guiseppe Ricciotti, *The Life of Christ* (Milwaukee: The Bruce Publishing Co., 1947).

turned to the twelve that were left and said, "Do you also want to go away."

Peter said, "Lord to whom shall we go. Thou hast the words of everlasting life. And we have come to believe and to know that thou art the Holy One of God."

At another time Christ told the Apostles not to be afraid, that after his death he would still be with them until the end of time, even though they could not see him.

The purpose of the Holy Eucharist as established at the Last Supper will be rightly interpreted as that Christ left the Holy Eucharist as a means for him to be present in a supernatural manner in Catholic churches all over the world.

When Christ established the Holy Eucharist at the Last Supper, he told the Apostles on breaking the unleavened bread, "Take and eat, This is My Body, which is being given for you, do this in remembrance of me."

A little while later, Christ took a chalice of wine mixed with water and having given thanks, he made all the apostles drink saying, "All of you drink this. The Cup is the new covenant of My blood, which is being shed for many."

Now if Christ meant his blood was being shed because of the sins of all people he would have said right out he was going to die because of the sins of all people. He would have said he was going to die in order to save them so that they could enter heaven when they died.

Christ would not have preached what he did, if he had died for our sins, to open heaven for us. Christ said to turn away from earthly things and pleasures and turn to God. Christ said you must have faith in God and trust Him.

During Christ's last discourse with the Apostles he said, "I will not leave you orphans; I will come to you. My peace I leave with you, my peace I give to you; not as the world gives do I give to you. Do not let your heart be troubled or be afraid." These words of Christ help prove that he would not leave the people of the world without his supernatural help.

Christ also told the people, "I bring you the New Testament." This can only mean that Christ did not come to prove the Old Testament.

The Gospels will be taken from the teachings of Christ himself. They will use Christ's own words that he used in teaching people about God in heaven.

Christ told the Pharisees and Sadducees, "The first commandment of all is the Lord our God is one God; and thou shalt love the Lord thy God with thy whole heart, and with thy whole soul, and with thy whole mind, and with thy whole strength. This is the first commandment. And the second is like it; Thou shalt love thy neighbor as thyself: There is no commandment greater than these."

The miracles Christ performed on earth will be explained in the Mass. These will illustrate the supernatural power Christ possesses to help people who have the necessary faith in Christ and God.

Thus the Mass of the future will be built around the creation of the Holy Eucharist by Christ and the crucifixion and resurrection of Christ from the dead because he was truly the Son of God and was a supernatural being.

Also the life of Christ will be explained in the Mass as much as possible. Such concentration will show that the mission of Christ on earth was to teach the people to have faith in God in heaven, to trust him and not fear Him; that Christ's mission was to have Peter establish churches; and that Christ created the Holy Eucharist as a means for him to be present in Catholic churches in a supernatural manner so that people could come to him for help.

During Christ's life on earth the main points in his teaching were:

1. God in heaven wanted people to know He wanted them to have faith and trust in Him.

2. Christ himself was the Son of God.

3. God's greatest commandment was to love God with your whole heart, with your whole mind, with your whole body, and with your whole soul.

4. The next commandment in importance was to love your neighbor as yourself.

5. Enemies were to be forgiven seven times seven and, yes, seventy times seven.

6. People should put their faith in God and not in earthly possessions and achievements.

7. The Last Supper and the Holy Eucharist were keystones of faith.

8. Peter was to be the first pope and that Peter and the other Apostles were to establish the Catholic Church and teach all nations what he had taught them.

9. Christ would die on the cross.

10. Christ would be resurrected from the dead in three days.

11. Christ would appear before the Apostles after his resurrection.

12. Christ's reassurance that he would be with the Apostles in a supernatural way, even though they could not actually see him.

The statements that Christ made to Peter and the other Apostles in regard to the leadership and powers of the Church meant that Christ had absolute confidence in Peter and the Apostles in their building of the churches and their teaching of the people about God.

Because God and Christ wanted the Catholic Church to survive, it has survived and will continue to exist in spite of all the human mistakes that the church leaders have made in Catholic belief and doctrine.

Church ceremony has been built around the Holy Eucharist or Blessed Sacrament. This is the direct means Christ established in order to give people a chance to seek his help right here on earth day by day.

Christ made it understood he wanted Peter and the succeeding popes to operate the Church with full authority from Christ himself.

Christ made it very clear that people had to have faith in God in order to receive a reward after death. Also it is absolutely necessary for people to submit their will to God's will.

In order to help people, Christ must be on earth someplace where people can go and get help through faith and submission of their wills to Christ himself. It is Christ and God who have the supernatural power to help people on earth.

Therefore the real fulfillment of Christ's mission on earth can only be accomplished through the Holy Eucharist or Blessed Sacrament in the Catholic churches all over the world.

CHAPTER NINE

How the Church Will Help People Solve Problems

After Church leaders recognize the truth that Christ is actually present in the Blessed Sacrament of the Altar, they can begin to plan their work in helping people to understand what Christ in a supernatural manner, will do to help them. Church leaders will understand their duty is to help people seek the help of Christ in the Blessed Sacrament.

Let us examine problems people face in life on earth and the way the Church of the future will solve them.

1. The goal In Life

What should a person consider his most important objective in life?

Church doctrine will state that living according to the plan that God has for each individual is of greatest importance. Since God controls a human being so completely during his life on earth, man has no reasonable choice but to try to follow God's plan for him. Man's total dependence on God is shown in the following ways:

First, no human being can choose who his father and mother will be.

Second, he has no choice concerning his creation and birth.

Third, he has no choice about how he will be raised and trained by his parents or other people.

Fourth, by the time he is old enough to take care of himself, he has already established habits of living that will help or harm him during the rest of his life. He has been trained rightly or wrongly by someone else.

Fifth, in spite of the best training he could have received in his childhood, a person still has no idea what his life will be like or what will happen.

Now, how can a weak and ignorant human being understand what God has planned for his individual life? He can look back and understand that since God has had absolute control over his life so far, God must have a definite reason for his life to be just exactly as it is. So it doesn't make any difference whether his life appears to be good or bad, God still has control and has His reason for allowing this person's life to be exactly as it is. God's only reason is to help His weak and ignorant creatures through this life and finally to their reward after death.

Thus a person who understands that his life is what it is, not because of his own free will and choice, but due to circumstances beyond his control, will accept his life right up to the minute just exactly as it is. When we accept life and ourselves exactly as they are, this means we are accepting the will of God, because God has absolute control over everything that happens on earth. If God does not interfere with events of our life, it means God has allowed our life to be as it is.

When a person can say to Christ or God, "I accept my life just as I find it to be. I am satisfied, even if it seems as if my training could have been much better. I know I can trust you and God; therefore, I put my faith in you. There is no other place on earth to come but to your dear Jesus in the Blessed Sacrament of the Altar. No human being can help like your supernatural help. Dear Jesus, if you can accept my plea for help, I certainly can accept the wonderful help you can and will give me."

Therefore, a person's goal in life must be to establish and keep faith in Christ and God. We can go to Christ in the Blessed Sacrament of the Altar and ask his help in choosing the work we do for a living. We can ask Christ for help in doing a good day's work at our job. We can ask his help in getting promotions and better wages, but we must take whatever comes, even if things seem to go against us, because Christ will never let anything happen but what is best for us. If we lose one thing Christ will help us get something better if only we accept his will and take what comes.

We must remember Christ is our best friend and he will not let us down or fail to do what is best for us.

It is by accepting what God allows to happen to us during our life, that we prove our faith in Christ and God. We certainly are submitting to God's will when we accept, without question, the things we don't like or don't understand.

A person can either fight against the happenings in his life, or he can accept whatever happens as being in accordance with God's plan for his life.

It is the seeking of help of Christ in the Blessed Sacrament before we make important decisions that saves people misery and suffering in life.

When you pray for guidance you can know with absolute certainty that Christ and God will allow only whatever is best to happen. If you get what you are seeking you will know it is according to God's will.

If you don't get what you want, you can know absolutely that God has something better in store for you, but you must have patience with God.

2. The Problem of Marriage

The Church will establish a recommended program for a man and woman to follow in deciding to get married or not.

a.) A six-month period of time will be required to get married in the Church. During this time the man and woman will study, with the help of the priest, the responsibilities of married life, and especially the understanding about raising and training any children from the marriage.

b.) Each week the priest, the man, and the woman will make a thirty-minute visit to the altar of the Blessed Sacrament, asking for help and guidance in regard to the marriage.

When a man and woman who wish to be married go to the church and ask Christ himself for help in making the decision about marriage, Christ will guide them in making the right decision. Each person will have a feeling of satisfaction from having left it up to Christ himself to guide him as to whether or not he should get married. Six months will give each party a good chance to find out if he or she is adaptable to or suitable for the other one. Since it is the hasty marriage that does not succeed in many cases, this six-months' program before marriage will help some people find out if they are truly interested in marriage, and thereby save themselves a lot of trouble.

3. *Teenagers and Their Problems*

The Church will work out a program to help teenagers in their difficult years of changing from childhood to adult life.

a.) The priests will be well trained in helping teenagers understand that their problems are common to all human beings.

b.) The importance of dependence on Christ and God will be taught by the priests. This means that teenagers will be encouraged to seek the help of Christ and God.

It also means that their minds will be trained to make themselves do what they know is best in every decision, small or great.

Dependability will help teenagers to help themselves; to make and keep good friends.

c.) Teenagers will be taught that marriage involves more than a boy and girl being in love with each other. It involves the responsibility of having a home and living together, the sacrifice that each one will have to make in order to be loyal to each other and to live together; the sacrifices that must be made to raise children they may have in marriage; and the cooperation that is necessary for husband and wife to work together and encourage each other when difficulties are found in marriage.

d.) Teenage groups will have weekly meetings for one-half hour visits to the Blessed Sacrament (with Christ there in a supernatural form) for silent prayer and adoration during which each teenager can ask Christ for help and guidance in his day-to-day problems.

e.) Each teenager will be taught to come to church and visit Christ in the Blessed Sacrament any time he has a problem and needs help and guidance. Thus, he will learn as a teenager that Christ is truly there to help him when he needs it so much.

f.) Teenagers will be taught by priests to have respect for other people, even if it means just letting them alone rather than condemning them or trying to change their ways. Time spent on self-improvement is always more valuable than time spent trying to change another person. The best way is to overlook the faults of other people. This does not mean we have to let others take advantage of us. It means we will stay away from people who are not treating us fairly. A very good time to go to the nearest Catholic church to visit with Christ in the Blessed Sacrament is when others aggravate us.

h.) Teenagers will be taught to have absolute faith in Christ in the Blessed Sacrament. They will learn by experience the wonderful help Christ will give them when they submit to the will of Christ and God. This is the help they will need every day of their life to be satisfied and happy.

i.) Teenagers will be taught that God is their goal in life and that there is no other place to go but to God at the end of their life on earth.

4. *Family Unity*

Parents and their children will be encouraged to make visits to Christ in the Blessed Sacrament. This will be very good to help promote family unity. Every member of the family will benefit by seeking the help and guidance of Christ and God.

5. *Personal Trouble*

Every Catholic will be told to come and visit the priest when he is in trouble. The priest will visit with the troubled person and then take him into the church where both priest and layman will silently pray to Christ for help and guidance. This way the priests can help many people learn to seek the help of Christ himself.

6. *Marital Happiness*

Married people will be taught to seek the help of Christ in the Blessed Sacrament. The priests will be of tremendous help in showing married couples how they can enrich their marriages by helping them to go and ask Christ for help and guidance when they need it.

CHAPTER TEN

The Effect of the New Belief in Christ on the Church Leaders

The leaders of the Church of the future will understand that the whole concept of religion must be changed to conform to the teachings of Christ himself.

Throughout the past history of religion, there seems to be the idea of atonement of sins by man to an unknown God. When tragedy struck people believed that the unknown God was angry with them for something they had done. They may not have known why their God was angry, or maybe they thought they knew why God was angry.

So we find that all types of sacrifices were offered up to God by followers of a particular religion. Usually it was their most prized possession. Human beings even murdered their own children as a sacrifice to an angry God. Many times a choice animal was sacrificed.

This kind of religion is not what Christ preached. Christ told his followers that it was not the Old Testament, but the New Testament he brought to them.

In the Church of the future, the Church leaders will accept what Christ taught about the commandments of God.

The first commandment of all was that the Lord thy God is one God, and that each should love the Lord Thy God with his whole heart, and with his whole mind, and with his whole strength.

Since Christ is the Son of God and is taking the place of

God on earth in a supernatural manner in the Holy Eucharist, the Church leaders have no choice but to teach the lay members of the church to learn to submit their wills to the will of God according to the first and greatest commandment. This also means submission to the will of Christ in the Holy Eucharist.

The second commandment was like the first one. Each should love his neighbor like himself. Christ said there were no other commandments greater than these.

These commandments certainly meant for human beings to submit their wills completely to the will of God. It meant for them to follow what God wants them to do as well as they are able.

This is exactly what Christ told people when he said he must do the will of his Father in heaven. This meant Christ was subject to God and must follow what God wanted him to do.

Christ told his followers he was the bread of life sent by God in heaven and unless they eat of Christ's body and drink of his blood they shall not have eternal life.

Instead of Christ telling the people he came to be crucified and die because of all their sins against God, Christ told them he came to give them his peace. This peace the world cannot give. He told them he would leave his peace with them and told them not to let their hearts be troubled or to be afraid.

These teachings of Christ are the beliefs that Church leaders must follow in bringing the people to Christ himself.

Christ in the Blessed Sacrament of the Altar is the source of help and guidance for all people.

It is the obligation of Church leaders to inspire people to build churches so that they will have a place of worship where Christ is present in the Holy Eucharist to help them.

It is the duty of Church leaders to teach people that

Christ is truly present in a supernatural manner in the Holy Eucharist.

They will teach the words of Christ that provide the understanding of the Last Supper's establishment of the Holy Eucharist by Christ.

Church leaders will teach the lay members that first, a person must be sincere in his prayers for help from Christ. Second, a person must accept whatever comes from his prayers. If his prayer is answered he will accept it as the will of Christ and God. If it is not, he must still accept it as the will of Christ and God. Third, the person must have faith, and believe that Christ knows what is best for him and will give him something else that is better yet. It is Christ and God who know what is best for each person, not any human being.

This is the way Church leaders will be doing their work for Christ and God.

There will be no dissension among Church leaders about any doctrines or belief set up by any Catholic leaders. There will be no trouble from Church members who think Catholic doctrines are wrong.

It will be Christ, himself, the people are seeking help from. If they are not satisfied with benefits they receive by asking Christ for help, they can tell Christ himself they are not satisfied. It is the obligation of Christ to help those who submit their wills to Christ and God.

If people truly submit their wills to Christ and God they will always thank Christ for his help and will never be disappointed. This is because Christ never makes a mistake when he helps people. People always get the best help from Christ and God.

Church leaders will find themselves free from the burden of responsibility in regard to benefits people receive from going to Church and seeking help from Christ and God. They can feel they have done their duty when they provide the church and the Holy Eucharist, and then use their efforts to get people to come to the church and ask Christ for the help they need so much. It does not make any difference what the problems of people may be, they can go with confidence and seek the help of Christ in the Holy Eucharist.

It will be the duty of priests and other church leaders to teach people that Christ and God will help them in any problems they ever face in life on earth.

Finally it will be the duty of the Church leaders to teach people to seek the help and guidance of Christ in anything they might want to do and in making any important decisions. It will be their duty to encourage people to ask for help before they get into problems. Christ will always guide them some way or other.

Church leaders will not be looked upon as dictators of what Catholics should do or should not do in order to be Catholics. They will be highly respected by people as their leaders, helping them to find Christ himself in the Holy Eucharist, to receive Christ's supernatural help.

The faith of the church members can be like that of the early Christians who would die rather than give up their faith and belief in Christ.

Church members will have no mistaken ideas about the motives of the priests and other leaders. They will not feel as though some members are treated better than others or favored more. They will not feel as thought the priest is angry with them for one thing or another.

The faith and confidence that will flow from the church members to their leaders will amaze them. All because they will have shown the members of the church how they will be helped by Christ himself.

CHAPTER ELEVEN

Christ Will Prove His Supernatural Presence

How Christ will prove to human beings that some way, unknown to them, he is actually present in a supernatural manner in the Holy Eucharist in Catholic churches all over the world is the most important question people face in their lifetime on earth.

The very first indication Christ gave to people that faith in God was absolutely necessary was through the miracles Christ performed. Christ always told people their faith in God, alone, would make a miracle possible.

Without faith, human beings cannot expect the help from Christ and God they need so much.

To prove to people he is actually present in a way people cannot understand, Christ told the Apostles at the Last Supper, "I give you my body and my blood. The wine is my blood and the bread is my body. Do this in commemoration of me. Unless you eat of my body and drink of my blood you shall not have eternal life."

With the Last Supper as a basis for the Holy Eucharist, it is up to people to go to the Catholic church and seek the help of Christ. If people seek in true sincerity and faith the help of Christ, then Christ has no choice but to help them.

The first thing people will be aware of is the quiet and peace that always is found where the Holy Eucharist is present (unless people are talking or making other noises). Usually very few people, or none at all, are present in church at off hours.

This quiet and peacefulness is very profound; it is a different world. There is not another place just like it because of the supernatural presence of Christ himself.

People do not have to be burdened with problems in order to enjoy a visit with Christ in the Holy Eucharist. Just go and sit in the church and relax. Tell Christ you are there to show him a little extra respect. It is impossible not to have a feeling of peace and mental satisfaction when you leave the church. It is a soul-satisfying experience.

People have a choice of living in a world full of earthly problems, dominated by people who are trying to live according to human standards; or they can put Christ and God right in the middle of their daily efforts, seeking the supernatural help that is so necessary.

Where else can people seek help and be absolutely sure they will always get the help that is best for them?

The only reason that Christ is present in a supernatural way in the Holy Eucharist is to help the weak and ignorant people God put on earth.

Is Christ obligated to provide every person with what he has asked for? No, Christ in fairness must not help an individual get something that is not good to have. Christ is obligated to help a person get what is best for him. Since Christ is a supernatural being, he will do what is best for anyone seeking his help.

Therefore any person seeking the help of Christ, must realize that if he doesn't get what he has sought help for, Christ, in his wisdom, will give him something better than what he prayed for.

Taking what Christ wants to give is submission of the human will to Christ and God's will.

During our lives on earth, many times people must submit their will to the will of other people, whether they want to or not. It certainly is easier to submit our will to Christ than it is to submit to the will of human beings.

Many times in our life Christ will give us the courage and strength to endure things which, without his help, would defeat us. By submitting our will to Christ and God's will, we receive the faith and confidence that carries us through our difficulties in life. We know at the time everything will turn out for the best. In this way Christ takes the worry and grief out of our difficulty. Whatever the problem, we can make a visit to the church and ask Christ for help.

Our prayer must be to ask Christ to do his will and God's will. We must pray for whatever is best to happen. Then we must accept what does happen. We can have the complete assurance that Christ and god will allow only the best for us. With this confidence in Christ and God there can be no disappointment in life.

It does not make any difference what happens, the help we receive from Christ himself will carry us through with confidence and lasting satisfaction in life.

Through the help Christ gives to people, he will prove to any human being—who keeps his faith in Christ—that some way he is present in a supernatural manner in the Holy Eucharist in all Catholic churches.

The final answer is that Christ will never fail to help those who ask for it. The one thing Christ demands is the submission of our will to God's will.